EYEWITNESS COMPANIONS

Guitar

RICHARD CHAPMAN

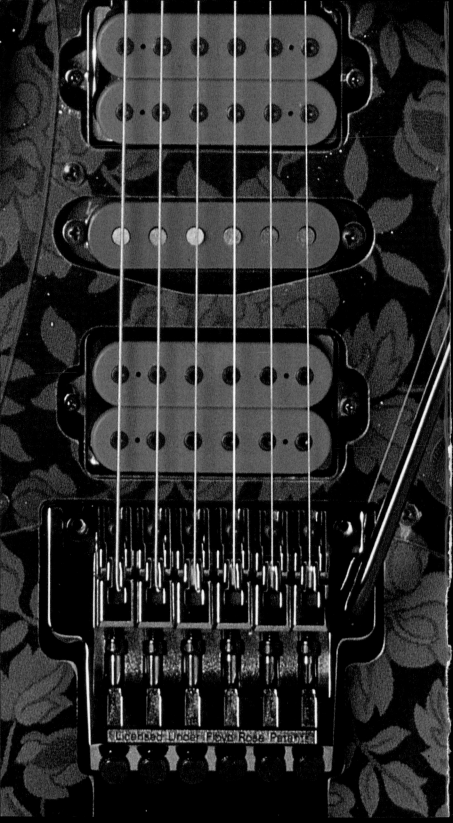

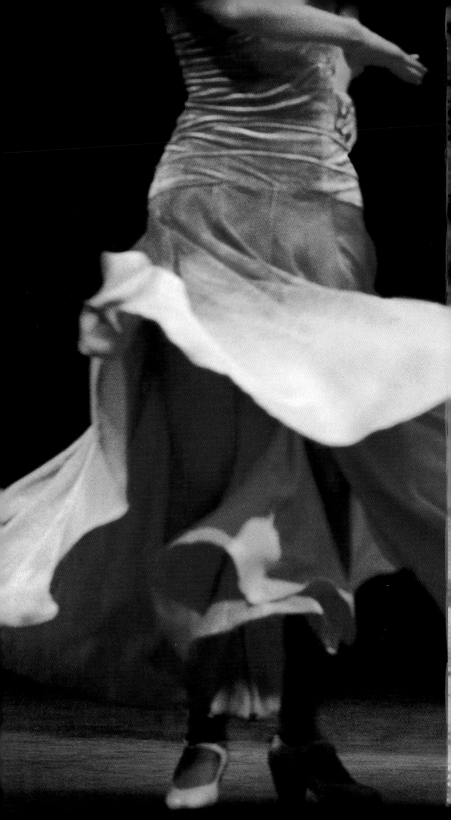

LONDON, NEW YORK,
MUNICH, MELBOURNE, DELHI

Art Editor	Jenisa Patel
Editor	Matthew Milton
Managing Editor	Miranda Smith
Managing Art Editor	Karen Self
Art Director	Bryn Walls
Publishing Director	Corinne Roberts
DTP Designer	Karen Constanti
Production Controller	Luca Frassinetti

Produced for Dorling Kindersley by
Project Editor Angela Baynham
Designer Edward Kinsey

First published in 2005 by
Dorling Kindersley Limited
80 Strand, London WC2R ORL

A Penguin Company

017-FD057-May/05
2 4 6 8 10 9 7 5 3 1

A CIP catalogue record for this book is
available from the British Library

ISBN 978 1 4053 0900 4

Colour reproduction by Colourscan,
Singapore
Printed and bound in China by
Leo Paper Products Ltd.

See our complete catalogue at
www.dk.com

CONTENTS

THE GUITAR IS USED FOR PLAYING ALMOST EVERY TYPE AND STYLE OF MUSIC. IT EXISTS TODAY IN A VARIETY OF FORMS, RANGING FROM SIMPLE NYLON STRING ACOUSTIC TO FUTURISTIC ELECTRIC MODELS WITH SOPHISTICATED ONBOARD ELECTRONICS.

Classical

The classical guitar has been in existence for more than 3,000 years. Early guitars had small bodies with four courses of gut strings and they were used in Europe to accompany songs and dances. Hardly audible for prominent musical roles, the guitar was used on its own to accompany singers and occasionally in small ensembles. It evolved acquiring a standard six-string in the third quarter of the 18th century tuning and a larger body in the mid 19th century. Today, the classical guitar is well established, and there is also a large repertoire of material written specifically for it, that ranges from early music to modern atonal compositions. The instrument continues to develop, with new arrangements and fresh works being written all the time. Technique has evolved over hundreds of years and tends to be orthodox. The great popularity of steel string acoustic and electric guitars has led to the classical guitar being somewhat overshadowed, yet the classical instrument is capable of producing some of the most appealing of all guitar music.

Spanish guitarist *Dioniso Aguado (1748–1849) produced a wide range of material for the guitar.*

Entry of the guitars
In the 16th century, the guitar was played both solo and in consort at all levels of society.

Flamenco

The classical guitar has always been closely associated with Spain and is still often referred to as the Spanish guitar. While the classical guitar and its music were developing in Spain in the 19th century, flamenco music derived from folk and Arabic traditions was also emerging in that country, with guitarists accompanying singers and dancers in a highly energized rhythmic style using scales and harmonies that have a Middle-Eastern flavour. Flamenco guitar playing became established in the 20th century, and although related to the classical guitar, it uses a whole range of different techniques including rasgueado strumming. Characteristic musical pieces that often have regional Spanish roots are played as a set of inventions with variations or as vehicles for improvisation. Flamenco exists both as a highly traditional form and as a modern evolving fusion, with South American and jazz influences.

This instrument, *made by René Voboam in Paris in 1641, is richly decorated with ivory and ebony.*

Blues

Based on African scales, rhythms, and inflections, and evolving within church music and other European influences, blues was the music of Afro-Americans, and its highly expressive power and immediacy came into focus with the guitar in the 1920s and 1930s. Acoustic styles on steel string guitars, with percussive picking and exotic slide techniques, were used to support emotional lyrics. In the 1940s, blues began to be played on electric guitars, and riffs, solos, and chords were melded to form a singular vocabulary that is catchy, appealing, and highly poignant. This in turn helped to pave the way for rock 'n' roll and the explosion of pop and rock developments in the 1960s. Blues still exists as a music in its own right and as part of the template for much of today's popular music on the guitar.

Country and folk

The unique identity and flavour of country music evolved in the USA, from roots that derived partly from British and European folk music. Songs and dances were accompanied by sophisticated fingerstyle techniques on acoustic steel string guitars. Fast virtuoso fiddle and banjo styles helped to lay the foundations for playing styles such as bluegrass. The electric guitar slowly became popular after the 1940s, and virtuoso country-style chord melody

The musically sensitive *French guitarist Ida Presti (1924–67) played in a duo with Alexandro Lagona (1929–99) and made outstanding recordings.*

and electric soloing started to emerge. Today, country is a diverse music, with both traditional and rock influences.

In North America, folk guitar styles were almost indistinguishable from country until the 1950s and 1960s, when the guitar started to be seen as a vehicle to accompany singer-songwriters. Folk also produced an interesting and diverse range of guitarists in Britain, where the guitar was considered a new vehicle for reviving lost traditions, as well as a way of exploring indigenous styles from around the world. On the electric guitar, folk rock emerged as a vibrant synthesis of tradition and innovation. In recent years, folk has spread around the world to explore and reveal a heritage of indigenous cultures on acoustic and electric guitars.

Gillian Welch (b.1967) *plays the guitar in a particularly sensitive way to support her crossover folk- and country-style songs.*

Jazz

The word jazz has come to be seen as an umbrella term for a wide range of musical styles that range from Dixieland to the avant-garde. Originating in the USA and linked to blues, ragtime, and classical music, early acoustic jazz styles with rich harmonies and virtuosic pick techniques emerged in the 1920s and 1930s. The invention of the electric guitar in the USA in the 1930s led to the guitar becoming an instrument that could rival the saxophone, trumpet, and piano when played in a group.

Jazz developed at an astonishing pace, from swing to bebop and modal areas, and the guitar

absorbed ideas from other instruments. It has been used for many years to realize advanced musical concepts, with compelling harmonies, complex linear solos, and open improvisation. Jazz has produced many of the greatest guitarists in the last 100 years, and with its multi-level stylistic crossover areas and futuristic experiments, it continues to lead the way in musical development.

Rock and pop

Today, the electric guitar maintains an unfailing appeal to every generation. This is largely due to the advent of rock 'n' roll in the 1950s and pop and rock in the 1960s, which led to the guitar dominating large areas of the world of music. The electric guitar in rock 'n' roll merged blues, country, and pop influences to become highly potent, and it has continued to form the basis for the launch of innumerable guitar-based groups. Amplifiers and effects such as echo and distortion are used to enhance the sound, and the guitar continues to create entrancing and infectious rhythms, harmonies, and melodies, and soaring solos that give the instrument a charismatic and seductive power.

Today in pop and rock, there are various approaches with roots in blues, rock 'n' roll, pop, soul, funk, and other hybrid and world music areas. Solos can be based on simple melodies, blues-based

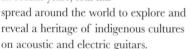

Today, the electric guitar still maintains an unfailing appeal to every generation

Buddy Guy (b.1936), *the great American blues guitarist, uses a Fender Stratocaster to create a range of emotional solos and fills.*

pentatonic vocabulary, classical ideas or jazz. And it is still appealing to back vocals simply with basic chords. In recent decades, synthesizers, midi, and computer-generated sounds have opened up unlimited possibilities for playing "sonic" guitar parts, where sounds and textures can be created that range from mimicking other instruments to unearthly futuristic soundcscapes. Today, rock and pop is played on both steel string acoustic and electric guitars, with pick and fingerstyle techniques and a wide range of styles and approaches, and it continues to be hugely popular.

I recommend the guitar as a wonderful medium for personal expression and fulfillment

guitar has been an essential passion and a life-enhancing occupation. The possibilities for musical development and invention have never ceased to increase. I could not imagine life without the guitar. It has been a matrix for connections and a touchstone that has given my life meaning. Inspired at first by jazz musicians such as Eric Dolphy and John Coltrane, and classical composers including Claude Debussy and Belà Bartok, I often found guitar music limited and stylized. Today, I have come to realize that the guitar has incredible potential and unlimited possibilities and I like to remind myself of that every day.

Playing the guitar

I recommend the guitar as a wonderful medium for personal expression and fulfillment, or even just as an object for simple enjoyment. For me, playing the

A big country star, *Garth Brooks has brought country music into the pop mainstream in the 1990s.*

RICHARD CHAPMAN

One of the biggest rock bands *in the world today, the Red Hot Chili Peppers were originally formed in Los Angeles in 1983. Guitarist John Frusciante (b.1970) joined the band in 1988.*